CW00671305

Berliners

A Dark Angels poem

by John Simmons

Images by

Andrzej Krauze

Paekakariki Press

2024

This is number **127**
of an edition of 250 copies

Isbn: 978-1908133-60-1

To Thérèse Kieran
Die bessere Handwerkerin
and Catherine Ann Berger
Eine Inspiration

Typeset in 12pt Monotype Garamond 156
and printed at Paekakariki Press, Walthamstow
on 120gsm Fedrigoni Arena Ivory Smooth

The Fire of Books

Berlin streets point forward and back. Now
I wander in the present tense while
crossing borders in the invisible past.

Let me see

Unter den Linden beckons straight ahead.
It would have me believe that here,
here in this café, Einstein took coffee.

Oh let us see

Did they widen the streets to allow
the ghosts to glide through more easily?
In a time that's now but reminds of then.

Let's see, come here

Two old men sip everlasting coffee
beneath hats, moving pieces around the board,
taking turns to exchange silence.

East and West brother

Woher kommen sie? It's a question
for a crystal ball to see the past that
brings us here and now and once upon a time.

Raising a hat to each other

*

In the East street
named Karl Marx
the workers march
their anger sparked
by paltry pay
despair damped down

by whispering fists
of Stasi in doorways.

Take your turn, then I'll take mine,
before we know it, we'll have passed the time.
The chess player looked at his Czech mate
who saw what was coming a touch too late.

Earlier, or perhaps later,
the American president came to claim
we are all Berliners.

Some scoffed at his doughnut error
but mark this, JFK mouthed the truth,
we *are* all Berliners.

We carry the marks of history
through the streets of this city,
we let the present pass by
with intimations of the past,
we nod at the past with echoes of the future.

*

Just off Kurfürstendamm
I rummaged in the deepest shadows of a shop
among the darkling *bric à brac*
where behind the stack of dusty books
gleamed the light of a crystal ball.

I took a look
and could see not what is to come
but what is gone. What was it?
Was?

Like a looter on the morning after *Kristallnacht,*
I tucked my treasure under my arm and ran and ran.

Let us see, let us see, under the bulb-naked light,
for seeing is not just believing but knowing
more than eyes can tell.

I see the Kaiser prepare for war
I see the trenches full of rats and mud
I see boots trampling on the torchlit floor
I see open mouths kicked shut with blood
I see windows smashed to jaggedeens
I see bunkers buried under rubble
I see peace that wonders what peace means
I see trouble.

I see a wall rising overnight
bringing darkness at first light,
I see the century parade in plain sight.

I hear children calling *fight fight fight*.

Like all of us I carry the past inside myself
sometimes squeezing into guilty margins of being;
being itself like this morning's *Frühstück* bacon
caught between the teeth, the stuck pig of history.

*

I see Frau Müller went blind,
unforeseen consequence of book burning,
playing for high stakes and losing
but consoling herself by seeing
the lower deck of what's still to come.

Oh she could still hear the tramp tramp tramp
of feet marching with boots shining

together and together and together
as slogans of hate infused her mind
with love of another kind.

Beneath the table she turns the card unseen,
it's for you, she says, though you might pass it on.
Pass it on, someone will know what to do,
even if that someone might not be you.

It is history, *Liebling,* I am giving you,
on another morning it will come true.

Take your turn, then I'll take mine,
before we know it, we'll have passed the time.

*

Each night in the bunker,
coughing in wreaths of candle smoke,
Goebbels read Prussian history aloud to Hitler,
Oh, to have led such lives!

And drinking water from a goblet,
finding comfort in the turning
of cards, staring at stars,
Imagine, just imagine!

To see the future that never arrived,
forever shrouded in clouds,
yet still there was something,
this something that survived.

In the last days they caught cockroaches,
waved a wand, turned them into coaches, until
they scuttled away, one smoky midnight,
through the rubble, leaving the dead behind.

Once I smoked.
Once, earlier this century I smoked
and loved to watch the drift
of smoke twisting from a cigarette,
rising like incense
into the night-time sky,
the sky dotted with stars
telling the story of the future,
but they burned all the books
to ashes and dust and the stars
fell out of the sky.

*

Herr Issyvoo also burned his past,
sweeping the inky remnants of diaries
into printed stories of what seemed more true,
making us laugh and smile and dance around
the cabaret's pretty boys who stepped out
as men doomed for things banned or burned
sliding off the sloping bookshelves
in the name of education
'men of books to men of character'
into the jaws of nazification.

*

There is an arsonist inside us all.
Perhaps a deep buried link
passing through the firelight
to times once spent in caves
the joy of sudden revelation
the spark that thrills
the fear it kills
the death of darkness.
Humanity's hand graffitied on a wall.

*

Now here they came.
Look into the crystal ball,
the past was always to blame.

The books were there for staking.
Now here the future came.
A monument in the making.

Young men, students
(or were they just thugs?)
jaunty in caps of purple and green
piled banned books high
                  in Opernplatz.

Hang them! Hang the Jews!
Burn them! Burn the books!
Higher and higher rose
the tower of Bebelplatz.

Who struck the first match?
We did, they said it, he struck it.
And now we watched what came next.

Flames leapt into darkness.
Sparks and specks of soot.

Dirt on a white shirt.

Flames leaping into darkness.
Sparks and specks of soot.

Who strikes the first match?
We do, they say it, he strikes it.
And now we watch what's next.

Hang them! Hang the Jews!
Burn them! Burn the books!
Higher and higher rises
the tower of Bebelplatz.

Young men, students
(or are they just thugs?)
jaunty in caps of purple and green
pile banned books high
                in Opernplatz.

Now here they come.
Look into the crystal ball,
the past is always to blame.

The books are there for staking.
Now here the future comes.
A monument in the making.

Above and Below

Dead fingers dig holes
in dead soil; constructing new
channels on West side,
burrowing to make tunnels;
East side thinks about a wall.

The rise and fall and
rise once more; on the tide of
its story, Berlin
sweeps along again, ready
to ride the next secret wave.

West side went under
inch by inch, miners digging
to listen unheard
while, unknown to them, George Blake
already played the betrayer.

Bought by pieces of
silver or turning the coat
of faith, did it matter?
Mutual assured destruction
rules in the playground bombsite.

Tunnellers, like moles
busied in blind intent, forged
ahead until one
day their ears and eyes lodged in
the rooms above, dishing dirt.

But the century
had not yet finished what was
there to hear and see,
the crystal ball showed the wall
where future bodies would fall.

In a dance of death
locked in an iron embrace
they held each other so tight,
scared what uncontrolled feeling
sudden release might unleash.

Rubbing their eyes and
covering their ears against
the clash of ideas,
dissonant, dissident and
dying of disappointment.

So stalemate set in.
Which side are you on, my boys,
which side are you on?
but there's nothing to be done,
girls, just nothing to be done.

One dark night, working
like Stakhanovites until
dawn's first light, East built
a thing of wonder, a wall
to keep two sides asunder.

The new day brought a
blank wall, a wall on which, at
risk of death, you could
paint your way—*Tschüss*—to your own
dark funeral in Berlin.

A young girl dawning
takes history's bony hand
that morning, and goes
for a walk as lovers do,
finding only no-way-through.

She came to the wall
and everything halted
while wide-eyed neighbours
gazed at narrowed vistas, scratched
heads in sudden disbelief.

A wall that shouted
turn back now, go back, go back
where you came. In high
sentry towers, staring down,
machine guns dared chicken runs.

In time, no time at all,
some made the run, from one *Zeit*
to the other, some
gunned down in no-man's-land,
others stood witness to dying.

Spies out in the cold
eyed the lofty lookout points
spaced along the wall,
and dug down deeper under
ground where frost lay thick and white.

Above ground S-bahn
trains found new routes, colours of
maroon and beige cast
into a gunmetal world,
sealed in time, waiting rebirth.

In the train station
until the big reveal of
future time, adverts
filmed over with nostalgic
dust from a frozen lost age.

Splash your way through tides
of history, pick seashells
from the platform shore.
Step back now, let memories
of the living past pass by.

Where everything
is broken, where decay rubs
shoulders with ruin,
everything is possessed of
an unintended beauty.

There is a presence
in today's denied absence,
a feeling missing
the being of yesterday.
But life comes to life again.

Life's alive again
because despite entrances
and exits off stage
something remains there
long after love's departed.

Silent angels walk
unnoticed here, felt not seen,
folding their wings of
desire, observing stories
of the city's ghost people.

'How can you live in
Berlin if you know any
of its history?
How can any walk these streets
knowing what once happened here?'

Step into this church
Marienkirche gloom-bright
in rubble's sunlight,
its darkest secret concealed
until time at last revealed

Beneath the whitewash
behind the glass, behold its
Totentanz, the *danse*
macabre of death, where peasants
hold hands with corpses and kings.

Something happens here,
some thought beyond living reach,
a grasping of hands
that dare not touch, yet longing
for what one day might still be.

Wir sind auch das Volk.
The *Wessis* and *Ossis* danced
together that day
knocking down the wall that had
kept their hands apart and dead.

Rejoicing on ground
without a city wall, hands
twined, footprints mingled,
hammer and pickaxe angled,
making a whole new vista.

A cellist played Bach
to the sound of bricks brought back
down to earth, while crowds
gathered in Alexanderplatz,
their eyes once dry now welling.

Through the streets the crowds
in one movement surge from east,
west round east again
trampling underground today's
silent dreams of yesterday.

As above, so below;
earth's alchemy turns to gold,
Else's wings spread wide,
uniting the old city,
Tiergarten's new Victory.

The Air of Deception

A scientist belongs to the world
at time of peace;
to his country at time of war.
So the military-industrial
complex was conceived by force of logic.

When the scientist connected thoughts
with the emperor
whose ideas ran only to war,
a fuse was lit by the spark,
blew lights out all over Europe.

Kaiser Wilhelm made his promise
and he made it standing at ease.
You'll be home
before the leaves have fallen, lads.
They all felt so jolly to be off to war.

The Kaiser had dreams that turned
into the waking nightmares of others.
He woke at night
and there, bathed in sweat and candlelight,
he snuffed out their hopes of peace.

*

The Kaiser dreams of railways,
the power they bring, transporting
oil from Arabia.

Some men's dreams never fade,
unbound by tracks of night and day,
some dreams never go away.

Kaiser Wilhelm's dreams extend
to Baghdad and beyond, oiling
wheels from Arabia.

*

Haber made bread from the air,
they said.
The chemist had mastered the art of war,
they said.

Under pressure, his own,
he made ammonia from nitrogen in air,
ammonia to fertilise the crops that made
the bread, so he made bread from the air,
they said, and then he made the gas,
gas the uniform colour of mustard seed,
turning soldiers into corpses deadening the ground
and he wore his invention with an air of pride,
with his heart dying on his sleeve.

*

Elsewhere, in the muddy trenches,
the little corporal gasped for breath,
rubbed his stinging eyes,
gassed into a lifelong fury.

After, there's silence in the woods,
the silence of birdsong.
A railway carriage
in sidings among the trees.
The victors make the losers
wait for the stationary train.

At Versailles the victors rub
losers' noses in the mud of defeat.
All war ends in silence
until the next one begins.

Retrace his footsteps, follow the track,
the track leading to the front,
stopping along the way at Chlorine,
then sidetracked to Arsenic,
next on to Mustard Gas,
the station decked out in yellow
as steam from the funnel
blew back into the angry face
of the corporal smeared in mud
and shit, in slime and blood,
slithering like a snake through the tunnel.

After the war
                          they pinned medals,
even the Nobel Prize to the chest
                          of Haber the chemist.

Such *Wunderwaffen*
                          killed thousands
and starved even more, their chemicals
                          blown on wind from farms,

from farms and fields
                          and forests to factories of war
So the train reversed
                          all the way east to Zyklon B

*

In the years that fall between,
in the elsewhen of banknotes
pushed along in wheelbarrows,
they are beguiled to laughter
by promises of land and bread,
bread dunked deep in blood
and toasted as freedom,
freedom you can taste in blood
spilled like beer, freedom you breathe
while drilling with the *Freikorps,*
filling lungs till giddy and drunk,
seeking freedom in death
yet instilled with the thrill of killing

*

The orders came from Berlin,
the orders led to this:

a rag-and-bone girl hugging a doll
in the corner of the carriage
while the train trundled through
the black-wooded night;

and her uncles played cards
on ghost bodies of the dead
where air is swapped for bread,
and blood pounds in wandering minds;

their hands sorted into best suits
as they dig with spades for diamonds,
as hearts still yearn for love,
and dreams are trumped and down-trodden;

by the joker who held all their aces,
by the dealer with the club foot.

*

The Führer dreams of railways,
the power they bring, carrying
Jews to Auschwitz
one way only
no returns.

Adolf Hitler's dreams descend
to the ticket office, charging
Jews for the ride
one way only
no returns.

*

They stepped down from the train,
shuffling down the platform,
bags in hand.

They passed through the gate,
ready to be made free,
ready to work.

They stood naked in the shower-room
embarrassed by their bodies
become so thin.

They walked, waiting for the slippery soap,
listened to the hissing, took a last
gasp of gas.

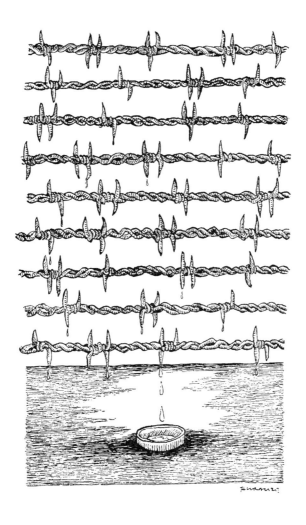

Reflections in Water

She dreams of white sheets and feather pillows,
lying there that time on grass beside the lake
above the sand, the ripples under the willows.

She wakes to icy splashes on her skin,
the sleep ungently washed from waking eyes,
she blinks to invite the new-day-sun within.

She dreams of being folded in her lover's arms,
the arms of another woman, such tears of joy
streaming at night with sounds but no alarms.

She wakes to sweat and dirt, lifting the sheet
once filled with roots, the sack that scrapes her skin,
that sags so light and thin, yet so dead a weight.

Another dream, rain-washed pavements shimmer,
a question hangs like lamps in drizzly night: Do you?
Of course. I love you still—*immer, liebchen, immer.*

*

In Berlin everyone is a symbol
of the past meeting the future
at a chequered checkpoint.

*

Josef stood his ground, making the effort
when really he just wanted to tumble

onto grass, entwine with his *Mischling,*
but the act of seeming strong held him upright

even after this last sleepless night with her,
this Jew he vowed never to see again.

There was a love-lorn mist hanging
over the lake.

Love once lost still kissed the dream
of love regained.

Lost love now lifts like cigarette smoke
from his fingers.

Smoke drifts away in light of morning
never reclaimed.

Here Josef gazed across the water,
longing to dance, one last time, with his forbidden love.

*

Later, a lifetime later, she sifted the sand
of her grandmother's life, following
the flow of records and memories
and stories that pointed her forever back
to this place, this house beside *Wannsee* lake.

There are times when history sends a shiver
of dread, anticipating what is next to come,
the reality of that day when uniforms in boots
clattered through the hall while they felt
the melting ice of murder on their tongues.

They knew, of course they always knew,
what their planning was leading to.

Even as they sipped coffee from china cups,
they shifted, caught between a sense of *etiquette*
and the forced labour of *bonhomie,*
foreign concepts surely for those insisting
on the purity of their immaculate vision.

Eyes blue and hair blond, their soul's longing,
they switched their gaze, unwilling
to catch their neighbour's glance, fearing
memories of a campfire's flames for boys
lying beside another lake in youthful days.

Water pure as life, unable to cleanse
the indelible stain of unforgivable sins.

Sitting there, around the polished table,
they might have seen their faces reflected
in the looming light of future guilt
they tried to scrub away ahead of time,
steeling their minds against the still-to-come.

For what they were about to do
they forgave themselves once they had signed
the paper, wrapping it in the language
and numbers of protocol, the death warrant
for millions, caught in the act of execution.

On the table the water jug stands,
tempting some to wash their hands.

*

There was nothing to be done, nothing
that could be undone by the force
of individual will, they took turns to swear
assent but mostly they just listened,
looked down, heads bowed, avoiding the eyes
of those who one day might bear witness
in the prosecuting trial of history.

Uncertain of her role—judge or jury
or pursuer of memory that might connect

between now and then—Anna could not find
the thread that made her a part
of her grandmother's tapestry,
the line that led from there to here.
Like Penelope she returned each day,
unpicking, pulling, sewing new stitches in time.

*

Across the lake
the trees are mirrored
on the surface of the water.

Reflection suggests there is another life
under this too solid one we count as real
eins zwei drei

the swimmer eases down into the water
thinking of Anna thinking of her
zehn elf zwölf

sun glinting on the rippling tide,
head ducking under
achtzehn neunzehn zwanzig

opening eyes, staring up
at the sun rising out of reach,
standing up, shaking water from hair.

Numbers are nothing
but an illusion of reality
seen on the surface of things.

*

Let us name her Anna and let Anna be for Berlin
the same seen from this side or from that

shouldering the unbearable burden of history
stumbling as she too felt the enormity of it all
like Atlas with the weight of the world on her back.

Elated.
      Agitated.

  *

She turned over, waking
from the deepest dream,
not knowing where she was
nor how she got there
nor who with.
            Anna rose from bed
standing at the window, seeing a shape
reflected behind her, a body breathing
beneath the covers, and from the balcony
observing the Spree meandering
past at a pace slower than history,
faster than time.
            There was a tree
just out of reach and on the tip of a leaf
a raindrop hung, poised on the point
of dropping, like a ripe fruit. *It's my time.*
She gazed at, then through it,
another crystal ball made for that moment,
the century's end.
            She watched
as from the blue-black sky a line of people
flowed into Tiergarten, surfing on stars
towards the column of gilded victory,
down the paths and between the branches,
around the ponds and through the animals

that once had been hunted here
among the ghosts of felled trees
buried into potato fields.
                    So now with linden
restored as if they'd never been cut away,
castaway refugees swept hither and thither
arm in arm, politicians with angels,
soldiers with cherubim, artists with seraphim,
the chess players and the book burners,
the teachers and learners and yearners,
the present, past and future,
the hope that is always last to die,
her mother and her mother and her mother,
floating on currents above the treetops,
sailing on a shining river of stars
down to an underground sea.

So the city lives
      so we all live in this city
so this city becomes the world
      and so, for a while, the world stops
as if pausing for something forgotten.

This is the way the world lives
      the millions who have been
this is the way the world lives
      the millions who wait to be.

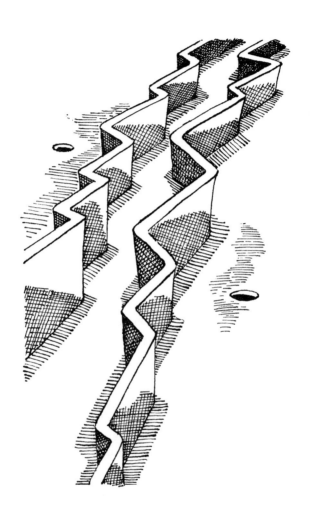